P9-CQF-400

MAKE it WORK!
PHOTOGRAPHY

Andrew Haslam

written by
Kathryn Senior

Photography: Jon Barnes
Consultant: Graham Peacock

World Book

in association with
TWO-CAN

MAKE it WORK!
Other titles

Published in the United States by
World Book, Inc., 233 N. Michigan Ave.
Suite 2000, Chicago, IL 60601
in association with Two-Can Publishing

Copyright © 1996 Two-Can Publishing Ltd.
Design © 1996 Andrew Haslam

**For information on other World Book products,
call 1-800-WORLDBK (967-5325), or
visit our Web site at http://www.worldbook.com**

ISBN: 0-7166-1731-5
LC: 96-60453

Printed in China

2 3 4 5 6 7 8 9 10 09 08 07 06 05 04 03 02 01 00

Editor: Robert Sved
Designer: Helen McDonagh
Project Editor: Kate Graham
Managing Editor: Christine Morley
Art Director: Carole Orbell
Series concept and design: Andrew Haslam and Wendy Baker
Additional photography: Ray Moller
U.S. Editor: Jeanne Johnson

Thanks also to: Katharine and Jonathan Bee, Sarah Martinez, James Davis,
Jamie Bignal, Thanujah Yogarajah, Ivan Lau, Louise Chan, Marisa Hawthorn
and everyone at Plough Studios.

Contents

Words marked in **bold** in the text are explained in the glossary.

Photography allows you to be a scientist and an artist at the same time. Most people take photographs to record events, but, by experimenting with a camera and making your own **prints**, you can create all sorts of different effects.

You will need

You can make the models in this book using simple materials such as balsa wood, cardboard, tape, and paper. For some projects, you will need to use small **lenses** that you can buy from model shops. Some materials are special to photography. Photographic solutions, photographic film and paper, film canisters, and film spools are all available from photography shops or large stores with photographic departments.

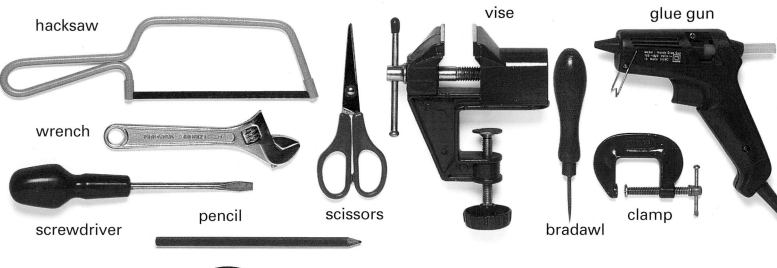

hacksaw · wrench · screwdriver · pencil · scissors · vise · glue gun · bradawl · clamp

drill · ruler

Photographers work in many areas: medicine and astronomy, as well as fashion, sports, news reporting, and in books and magazines.

MAKE it WORK!

Building the models in this book will show you some of the basic techniques needed to take photographs. You will see how light makes images on photographic paper and film, how different cameras work, and how you can develop and process your own photographs.

Cutting, drilling, and joining

You will need some tools to cut the materials. Measure each part accurately, marking with a pencil before cutting things out or drilling holes. Always cut away from your fingers. When you have cut wood, sand off any sharp edges with sandpaper. When you need to drill a hole, use a pointed bradawl to start the hole and then finish it off with a hand drill. A glue gun is useful for joining parts of models.

Safety!

Sharp tools are dangerous! Always take care and ask an adult to help you. Make sure that anything you drill is held firmly so that it does not slip. A small table vise is ideal for holding wood. Always use rubber gloves and tongs when working with photographic solutions.

watch · flashlight

Setting up a darkroom

Photographic paper is coated with chemicals that change when ordinary light falls on the paper, so you need to handle your paper in a darkroom with a red safety light. A small room with a sink makes an ideal darkroom. Cover windows with black garbage bags or black paper. Light the room with a flashlight covered with a red plastic **gel** or a lamp with a red light bulb. Fumes from photographic chemicals must not be inhaled for long periods of time, so take a break outside every 15 minutes.

Buying photographic paper and film

This book will help you decide what you need to use to make your prints. There are many types of paper and film to choose from, so make sure you know what kind of photographs you will be taking before you buy your equipment.

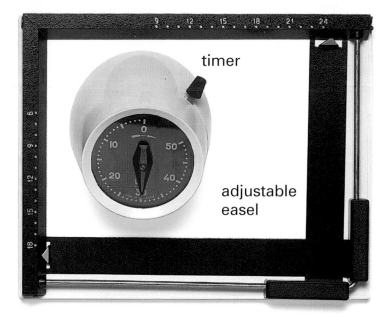

timer

adjustable easel

Making prints

To make your own photographs you will have to buy chemicals from a photographic shop. There are many different brands, and you will need to **dilute** most of them before use. Follow the manufacturer's dilution and temperature instructions carefully.

flashlight with red gel

rubber gloves

photographic paper

fixer

thermometer

measuring cylinder

tray   funnel   tongs

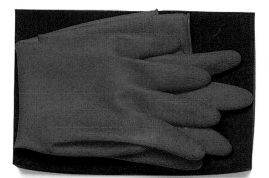

photographic film and canisters

developer

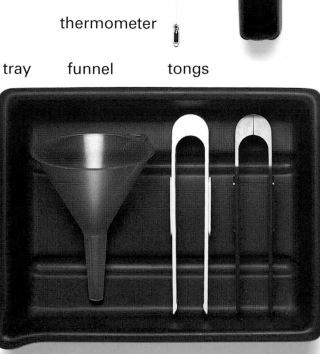

Light is a type of **energy** produced by the sun, electric light bulbs, and candles. In photography, light **reflected** from an object enters a camera through the lens. Where light hits the chemicals on the surface of photographic paper or film, an **image** is formed.

MAKE it WORK!
You can make a ray box and use it to investigate light.

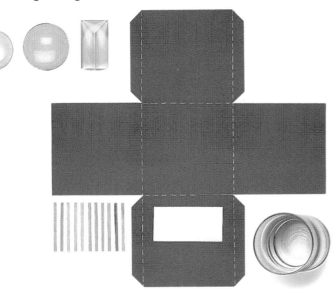

You will need
a 9-volt battery
scissors
a prism
lenses
glue

a craft knife and tape
balsa-wood strips 2" x $\frac{1}{8}$"
a small bulb and bulb holder
two paper clips and two wires
thin green and black cardboard
a glass of water and small mirror

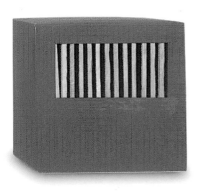

1 Cut out the cardboard as shown above. The square flaps should measure 4" x 4". Using a craft knife and with an adult's help, cut out the window. Score along the dotted lines.

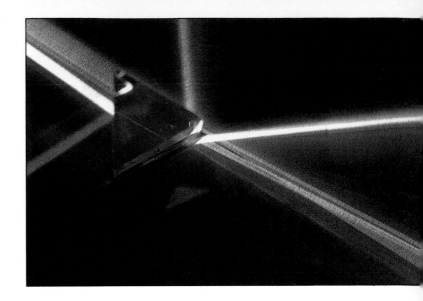

2 To make the grating, glue the balsa-wood strips over the window, as shown below left.

3 Fold the cardboard to form a box. The balsa-wood strips should be inside the box. Glue the flaps together using the tabs.

Using your ray box
Connect the bulb to the paper clips with two wires. Now attach one paper clip to each battery terminal. Make the room dark, and place the ray box over the bulb. You will see light spreading out in the shape of a fan. Notice that each light beam is a straight line. Light always travels in straight lines.

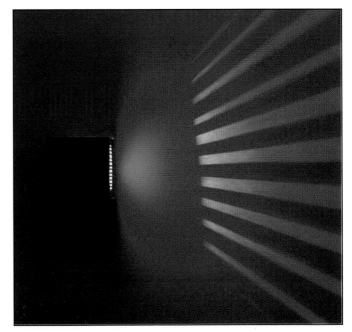

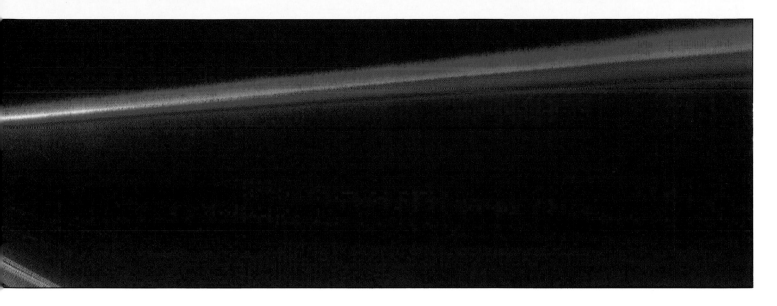

For these experiments, you will need to block off most of your grating. Fix two pieces of black cardboard inside your box with tape so that light can pass through only a small section of the grating. You will now see one or two beams of light.

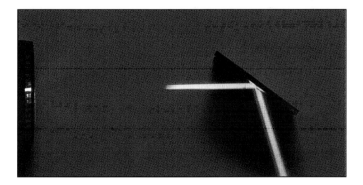

▲ Reflection

Look at the effect of shining a single beam of light into a mirror. Mirrors are very good reflectors of light. You should see that all the light that reaches the mirror is reflected back. Try changing the angle of the mirror and see what happens.

▲ Splitting white light

Light looks white, but really it is made up of many colors. Shine a light beam through a prism and you will see that white light splits into red, orange, yellow, green, blue, and violet light.

▼ Bending light

Light can pass through objects that are **transparent**, but not through objects that are **opaque**. Some transparent objects can cause a beam of light to **refract**. Shine a light beam through a glass of water. You can see that it does not travel straight through: the refracted beam is at an angle to the original.

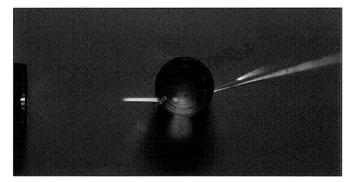

◀ Using lenses

If you pass light beams through a **convex lens**, the beams **focus** at a single point. The distance between the lens and this point is the focal length of the lens. As light travels in straight lines, the beams continue in their new direction traveling away from each other. What happens when you shine light through a **concave lens**?

You will need

two strips of thick balsa wood, $3/4$" x 10"
a piece of glass, 10" x 10" and a candle
a small lens in a round plastic holder
clay   a pencil
tracing paper   a mirror, 10" x $13^3/4$"
aluminum foil   Scotch tape and glue
thick cardboard   scissors and a craft knife

1 Cut the cardboard into the same shape as you did for the box on page 6. Each square flap should measure 10" x 10".

2 With an adult's help, use a craft knife to cut a circle the same size as the lens holder in the center of the top flap. Score the cardboard as before. Glue the flaps together using the tabs.

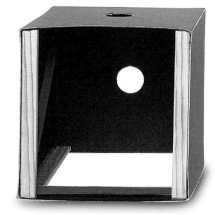

3 Put the mirror into the box, so that it lies diagonally across the box with the mirrored side facing the hole. In this picture, you can see the hole in the top reflected in the mirror.

4 Glue two balsa-wood strips to the sides of the open end.

The term *camera obscura* is Latin for "darkened chamber." In a camera obscura, light enters through a lens in one side. It is then reflected by a mirror forming an image on the screen at the top of the camera. There the image can be traced onto paper easily. These first cameras were used by artists for sketching views.

MAKE it WORK!
Use your own camera obscura to produce and trace an image of a candle.

5 Tape tracing paper to one side of the glass and place the glass, paper side down, on top of the wood strips. Tape it in place with Scotch tape. Squeeze the lens into the hole.

Experiments with your camera obscura

You will need to find a room with hard flooring. It is best to tape a piece of aluminum foil onto the floor to protect it from hot wax. Use clay to hold your candle securely in place.

Carefully light the candle and put the camera a short distance away. Use some dark cloth to cover your head and the camera, so that you can look at the screen at the top of the camera. Keep the material well away from the candle. You may need to move your camera back and forth, but you should be able to see a clear image of the candle on the screen.

Remember! Never leave a lit candle unattended.

Drawing the image

Tape another piece of tracing paper or some thin drawing paper over the screen. Now use a pencil to trace the image of the candle. Try using your camera obscura to draw other objects.

The camera obscura was first used in China in the seventh century. Alhazen, a 10th-century Arabian philosopher, used one to study the sun. The camera obscura was first described in detail in the 15th century by Leonardo da Vinci.

If you removed the mirror from the camera obscura, the image would appear, upside down, at the back of the camera. In a modern camera, photographic film lies across the back of the camera to record the image.

MAKE it WORK!

You can use a room that has only one small window to make a giant camera. If you move the position of the image in the giant camera you will see why modern cameras have their film fixed in one position. The following experiment works best on a sunny day.

You will need

an artist's easel or a chair with a piece of board
large sheets of black paper
pens and pencils   tape
white paper   a pin

1 Ask an adult to help you black out the window using black paper and tape. Use a pin to make a tiny hole in the center of the paper.

2 Set up the easel in the middle of the room. Tape some white paper onto the easel.

3 Make sure the room light is off. You may have to move the easel back and forth to get a clear image.

Looking at the image

The wall opposite your window should be filled with a giant, upside-down, or **inverted**, image of what is outside your window. A small part of the image should appear on the paper on your easel. Try moving your easel nearer and farther away from the window until the image on the paper is as clear as you can get it.

Change the angle of the board so that the left edge is nearer the window than the right. Draw the image that you see. Now do the same with the bottom edge nearer the window. How are these images different from the image made when the board is directly facing the window?

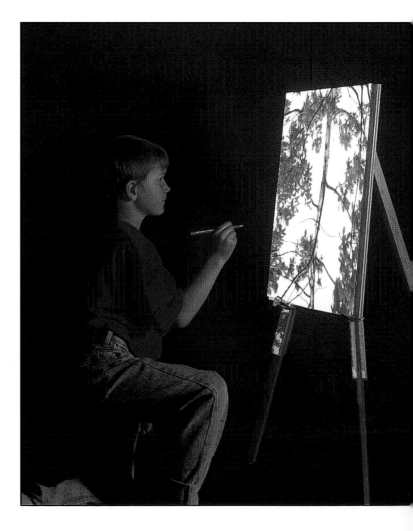

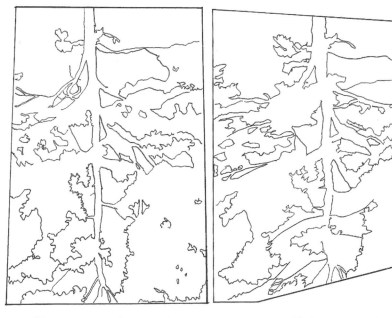

▲ To see your image in proportion, the paper must be directly facing the window.

▲ If the paper is kept upright but turned slightly to the left or right, your image will look wider.

◄ If you move your paper down so that it lies almost flat, the image will get longer and become very distorted.

Camera images

In a modern camera, photographic film sits inside the back of the camera so that it directly faces the lens. If the back of the camera is not flat, the image on the film will be distorted like the pictures of the tree shown above.

Why is the image inverted?

Light travels in straight lines. Some of the light that is reflected off the top of the object passes through the pinhole to the bottom of the wall. Some of the light from the bottom of the object passes through the pinhole to the top of the wall. In this way, light beams from all over the object travel through the pinhole in straight lines, forming an inverted image on the wall.

When light beams from an object enter your eye, they are focused by a lens onto the back of the eye forming an upside down image. So our eyes see everything upside down and it is our brain that turns the image the right way up.

12 Pinhole Cameras

The pinhole camera is the simplest camera you can use to take photographs. Light enters through a pinhole at one end of the camera and falls onto a piece of photographic paper at the other. When the paper is **developed**, an inverted **negative** image can be seen.

1 Cut the cardboard into the two shapes shown below. For your black base box, each square flap should measure 4". You will need to make your orange top box $\frac{1}{16}$" bigger all around so that it fits over the base box.

2 With an adult's help, use a craft knife to cut a $\frac{3}{4}$" diameter circle in the center of the bottom flap of the orange cardboard. Make a pinhole in the center of the corresponding flap in the black cardboard.

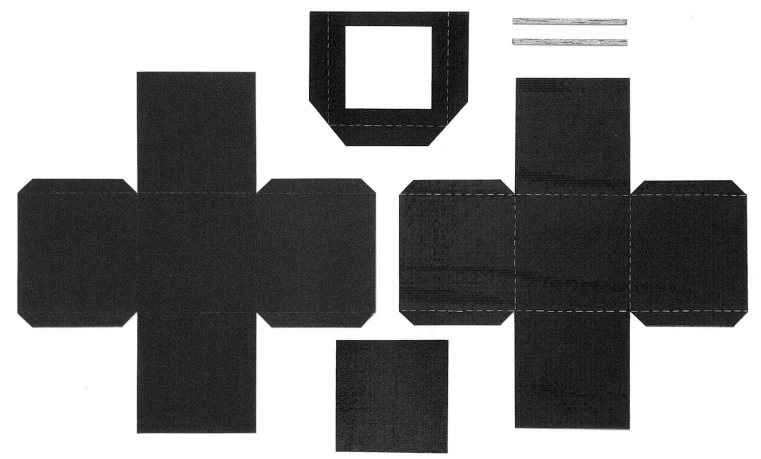

MAKE it WORK!

You can make a pinhole camera to take your own pictures using photographic paper. To load and unload your camera, you will need to use a darkroom.

You will need

thick black and orange cardboard	glue
two strips of balsa wood $\frac{1}{8}$" x 4"	tape
a craft knife	a pin
scissors	

3 Score along the dotted lines and glue your boxes together using the tabs.

4 For the photographic paper holder, cut a piece of black cardboard with tabs and a central window, as shown above. The dotted lines form a 4" square and the window is $3\frac{1}{4}$" square. Place a piece of card, 4" square, on top of the window. Fold the flaps up and tape them to the back of the square cardboard.

5 Place the paper holder in the back of the base box. The window must face the pinhole. Glue two balsa-wood strips inside the base box so that the paper holder will not fall forward.

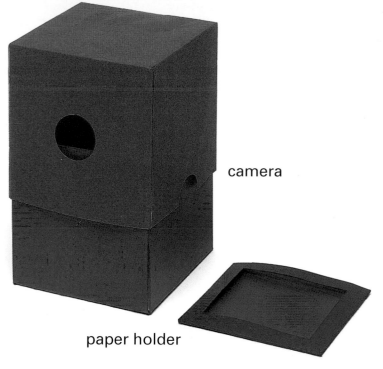

camera

paper holder

Finding something to photograph

Before you load your pinhole camera with photographic paper, you will need to find an object or scene to photograph. Try to find a bright scene that doesn't move. It is best to go outside or place your camera on a window ledge on a sunny day. You can also take pictures indoors by placing objects next to a window or by using lamps to light your scene. A scene with a strong **contrast** will produce a better print, so try to light your objects so that they produce shadows.

On pages 14-15 you will see how to load your camera and take pictures.

Look at pages 30-31 to see how to use a lamp and some cardboard to direct your lighting.

MAKE it WORK!

You are now ready to load your camera with photographic paper. Make sure that no ordinary light can enter your darkroom, and light the room with your safety light. You should try to touch the shiny side of the paper as little as possible.

You will need

a pinhole camera
photographic paper
a black light-proof box
scissors
safety light
a darkroom

Photographic paper

Photographic paper is a thick paper coated with light-sensitive chemicals called emulsion. The shiny side is the emulsion side. When light falls on the emulsion, the chemicals change to record an image.

Once you have **exposed** the photographic paper, you need to store it in a light-proof box. This keeps it from being spoiled until you develop the print. Make a box from black cardboard or paint a ready-made box black.

1 With your safety light on, take a piece of photographic paper from its box.

2 Cut the paper so that it fits into the paper holder. Touch the emulsion as little as possible.

3 Slide the paper, emulsion side toward you, into the paper holder.

4 Slide the paper holder back into position at the back of the camera so that the paper is facing the pinhole.

5 Put the lid back on your camera so that it rests about $3/4$" from the base, covering the pinhole.

*Light-sensitive paper was invented by William Fox Talbot in 1839. With one exposure, the paper produced a negative image from which many **positive** prints could be made. A friend of Talbot's called the invention "photography."*

You will find that some of your pictures are very pale images. These have been **under-exposed**. Others may be very dark. These have been **overexposed**. Make a note of the time needed for the best exposure.

Taking photographs

Now it's time to take some pictures. Put your camera in position in front of your scene. Make sure the camera is on a steady surface or attach it to a tripod (see pages 28-29). To make an exposure, push the lid all the way down. Pull the lid back up at the end of the exposure. You will need to experiment to find a good exposure time. Start by letting light into the camera for 15 seconds. Develop your print by following pages 36-37.

Try longer or shorter exposure times until the exposure on your final print is right. Reload your camera in a dark room for each exposure.

16 Focal Length

Every camera you buy today has a lens. When light enters a camera, all the light beams pass through the lens and change direction, as we saw on page 7. Although light enters the camera from many angles, the image will focus at a single point inside the camera. The distance between the lens and this point is called the focal length of the lens.

You will need

stiff wire   glue
cardboard   scissors
a bradawl   thin balsa wood
a craft knife   a dowel $1/4$" x 3"

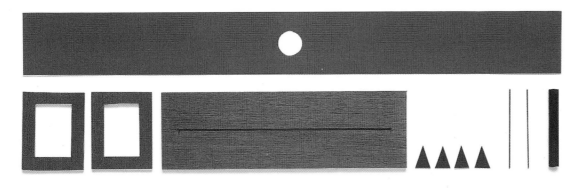

1 With an adult's help, use a craft knife to cut a $6^1/_4$" x 2" balsa-wood base, with a central slit $3/_8$" short of each end.

MAKE it WORK!

This viewfinder shows you how lenses with different focal lengths give different **fields of view**, without moving nearer or farther from the subject.

2 Cut two smaller pieces, both $2^1/_8$" wide and $1^3/_4$" high. Cut a window, $1^3/_8$" x 1" inside each rectangle.

3 Glue one rectangle to the end of the base. Push stiff wire through the frame of the other rectangle to make a cross. The wire from top to bottom should be $2^3/_4$" long, so that it pokes through the slit in the base. Use a bradawl to make a hole in the end of a thin dowel. Push the wire into the dowel to make a handle.

4 With scissors, cut a strip of cardboard $15^3/_4$" wide x $1^3/_4$" high with a hole in the center. Position the hole over the fixed window. Now glue the cardboard to the two windows and make folds, as shown above.

5 Make and glue cardboard arrows to the base $1^1/_2$", $2^1/_4$", $3^3/_8$", and $5^1/_8$" from the fixed end of the base. These distances give the fields of view of the lenses on the opposite page.

Using your viewfinder

a **wide-angle lens** with 18-mm focal length

35-mm lens

85-mm lens

105-mm **telephoto lens**

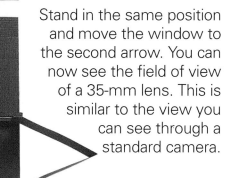

Position the window at the arrow nearest to you. Look through the circle. The field of view, as shown right, is the same as a wide-angle lens, left.

Stand in the same position and move the window to the second arrow. You can now see the field of view of a 35-mm lens. This is similar to the view you can see through a standard camera.

Move the window to the third arrow. You can now see what it is like to look through an 85-mm lens.

With the window at the final arrow you will see how close an image can appear with a telephoto lens.

When you look through a special lens, called a fish-eye lens, you can see everything within a 180° angle. Fish-eye lenses were originally developed so that scientists could take photographs of the sky when studying astronomy or forecasting the weather.

Getting even closer
Macro lenses can produce images larger than your subject. Macro lenses are used for taking close-ups and magnifying objects.

A zoom lens is one that can change its focal length. If you have a camera with a zoom, you can take photographs over a range of fields of view without having to change lenses. Many small cameras have zooms.

1 With an adult's help, cut the cardboard, thick cardboard, and plastic shapes shown. The black box should measure 4″ x 8″ x 6″ when complete. The red box is $^1/_{16}$″ larger all around.

2 Cut a $^3/_4$″ diameter circle in the center of the bottom flap of the red cardboard for the top box. Make a pinhole in the center of the corresponding flap in the black cardboard. Score along the dotted lines. Fold and glue the boxes using the tabs.

3 For your tripod attachment, cut a hole in the thick cardboard to fit the nut. Glue black cardboard over it to keep the nut in place and glue to the black box.

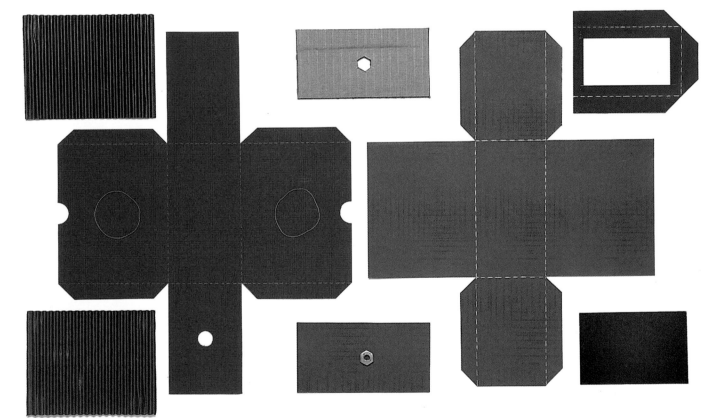

MAKE it WORK!

Pinhole cameras don't have lenses, but you can use a movable paper holder to see how different focal lengths give different fields of view.

You will need

photographic paper and a light-proof box, thick cardboard, a craft knife, scissors and glue a nut with $^1/_4$″ hole, a pin and two rubber bands, black corrugated plastic, red and black cardboard

4 Line your black box with two sheets of corrugated plastic. The grooves act as slots in which you can position your paper holder.

5 To make the paper holder, place a piece of black cardboard 4″ x 6″ on top of the black cardboard window. Fold the window flaps up and tape them to the back of the piece of black cardboard. You will need to load and unload your camera in a darkroom. To make your prints, see pages 36-37.

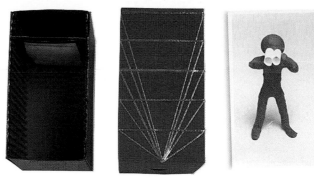

▲ With the paper near the pinhole, a wider field of view is produced; the image appears smaller.

▲ When the paper is farther from the pinhole, a smaller field of view is produced; the image appears larger.

Using your camera

Choose a scene to photograph and place the paper holder 4″ from the pinhole. You have already found out the best exposure time for this length on pages 14-15. Make the exposure.

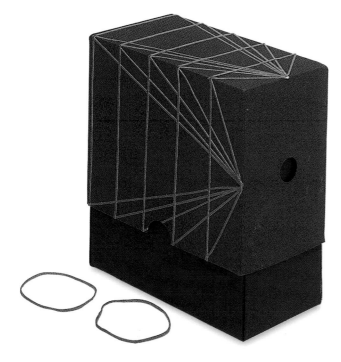

Unload the camera and keep your exposed paper in a light-proof box until you're ready to make your prints. Reload the camera and move the holder to a different position. When you increase the focal length, make your exposures slightly longer. Make prints to see the results.

Draw lines on your camera to show the angle of view at each setting. Keep your empty camera together with rubber bands.

Most cameras use film rather than paper. Film is a thin strip of material coated with light–sensitive chemicals. The dull side of the film is the emulsion side. Cameras take different sizes of film because they have different formats. The format is the area of film exposed to light when you take a photograph.

120-roll film

empty 120-film spool

Why film?

Using a camera that takes film rather than photographic paper has two advantages. As film is about 10 times more sensitive to light than photographic paper, you can take pictures using much shorter exposure times. This allows you to produce clearer shots, even when shooting moving objects. You can also enlarge and **crop** your image when you are making prints from film.

120-roll cameras

35-mm film

underwater
disposable camera

old folding camera

compact camera

Choosing a camera

All the cameras shown here are very common. Many of the older models can be bought cheaply from secondhand shops. You could use any of them, as well as the simple cameras that you can learn to make with this book, to practice photography.

Single-lens reflex cameras (SLRs)

When you look through most cameras, the view through the viewfinder is slightly different from the view through the lens. But an SLR camera has a mirror system so that you see exactly what will appear in your photograph.

SLR camera

compact with zoom

110 film

110 camera

Before film was invented, photographers had to use pieces of glass coated with chemicals that needed to be processed immediately. This meant that photographers had to carry a huge amount of equipment with them.

Buying film

You can buy all of the film sizes on this page, but you may need to go to a photographic store to buy 120 film. Once you know the format you need, you have to decide whether to use black and white or color film and also whether to use negative or **transparency film**. You will also notice that films have different **ASA** numbers. Film with an ASA number of 200 is twice as sensitive to light as film with an ASA of 100. With ASA 400 film you can take photographs indoors without a **flash**.

a 35-mm color negative

Formats

The format determines the shape of the final image. A 35-mm camera usually produces a rectangular view. The 120 and Polaroid cameras used here produce square views.

a 2" x 2" transparency produced by a 120-roll film camera

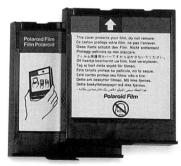

Polaroid film

Polaroid cameras

Polaroid cameras are very different from the other cameras shown here. They use special film that contains all the chemicals needed to process the image. A print is produced within minutes.

Polaroid cameras

a Polaroid print

The shutter and aperture are parts of the camera that control the amount of light entering it. The aperture is an adjustable hole at the front of the camera. The shutter controls the length of time that the aperture is open to allow light to pass onto the film. You can change the size of the aperture and the speed of the shutter to let the right amount of light into your camera.

MAKE it WORK!

Over the following pages you will see how to make a simple camera that uses film. The first stage is to make a shutter. By making a shutter with a fixed speed you can see how shutters work.

You will need

small pieces of wooden matchstick
$3/16$" thick balsa wood:
   one small block 1" x $3/8$"
   one rectangle $4^3/4$" x 3"
   two strips $4^3/4$" x $3/8$"
   two strips $2^1/2$" x $3/8$"
a compression hairspring
a selection of screws
thin brass 4" x 4"
black spray paint
tracing paper
a craft knife
a drill
glue

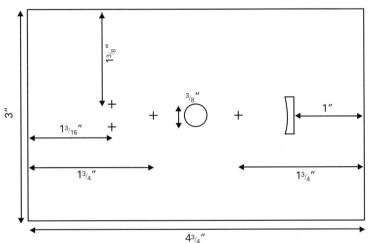

▼ Trace these shapes to make your brass pieces. With an adult's help, drill small holes where the crosses are marked and spray paint the pieces black.

▲ You will need to make holes and a slot on your balsa-wood rectangle as shown. The screw holes, marked as crosses, should only pass halfway through the board.

1 Glue balsa strips to the rectangle to make a shallow box. Paint the inside black. Place the keyhole-shaped piece of brass in position and screw it to the box. It should move from side to side. Fit two other screws to limit its movement.

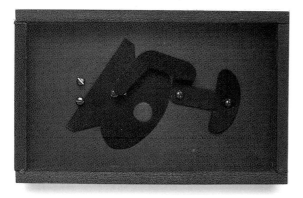

2 Screw the crooked brass shape into place using two more screws. You need to bend the middle section of the shape so that the lower part stands away from the board.

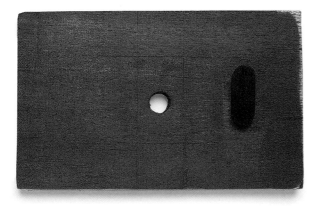

3 Fit a long screw through the hole at the end of the crooked shape. Pass it through the slot to the top side of the box and into the small block of balsa wood. This is the shutter release button.

4 Glue two tiny pieces of matchstick and the hairspring to the brass pieces so that the hairspring is attached to the underside of the crooked piece and the top of the keyhole piece. Let dry overnight.

Looking at the shutter
To release your shutter, slide the button across. You will see the spring tighten. The lower brass piece will move quickly across the hole. To release again, move the button the other way and the brass will slide back across.

Changing shutter speeds
The shutter you have made has a fixed speed. Most cameras can change their shutter speed. Using a fast shutter speed you can freeze moving objects. With a slow speed you can deliberately blur images.

▶ This photograph of a disk spinning on a motor is taken with a slow shutter speed of 1/8 of a second.

▶ This photograph is taken with a medium shutter speed of 1/60 of a second.

▶ This photograph is taken with a fast shutter speed of 1/1000 of a second.

Making the body of your camera

Like the camera obscura and pinhole camera, a modern camera is a box that only lets light in when the aperture is open. Most cameras have a lens at the front that focuses light onto the film at the back. You can build onto your shutter to make a camera that takes pictures. Ask an adult to help you cut all of these pieces.

3 For the top, **c**, and the bottom, **d**, of the camera, cut two rectangles of $1/2$" balsa wood, 1" x 5". Make a $3/8$" hole at one end of the top piece. At the other end make a hole the same size but only halfway through the wood. Do the same for the bottom piece. Paint the side with the half-made hole black for both the top and bottom.

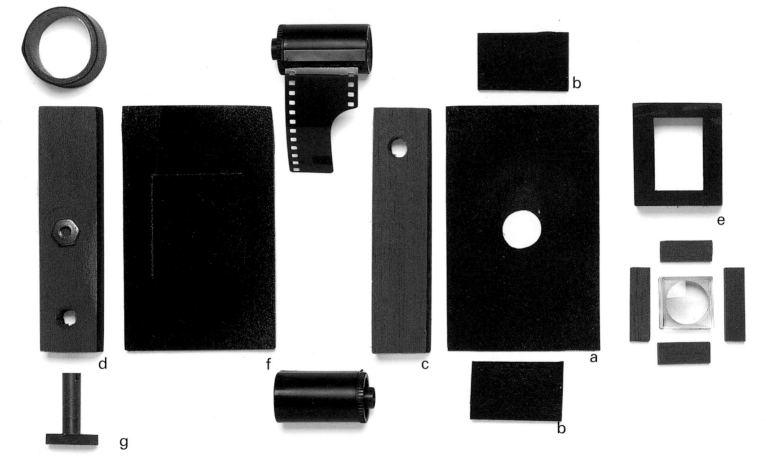

You will need

balsa wood: $1/16$", $3/16$", and $1/2$" thick
a small brass cylinder $1/4$" in diameter
black paint and a paintbrush · tape
strong double-sided tape · a saw
an empty film canister · a craft knife
a nut with a $1/4$" hole · a small lens
electrical tape · a roll of film

1 For the camera front, **a**, cut a 3" x 5" rectangle of $1/16$" balsa wood. Cut a $3/4$" hole in the center. Paint it black.

2 For the camera sides, **b**, cut two rectangles of $3/16$" balsa wood, 1" x $13/4$".

4 For the film frame, **e**, use four rectangles of $3/16$" balsa wood to make a frame measuring $13/4$" x 2" around the outside. The rectangles should be $2/3$" wide. Cut a $13/4$" x 2" piece of $1/16$" balsa wood with a 1" x $11/2$" central window. Glue this to the frame.

5 For the camera back, **f**, cut a 3" x 5" rectangle of $3/16$" balsa wood. Cut a $11/2$" square of $1/16$" balsa wood and glue it to the center of one side. Now paint this side black.

6 For the winder, **g**, saw two slots in the end of the cylinder so that it clips into the end of a film canister. Glue this to a piece of balsa wood.

7 Open the empty canister and tape the end of your film to the inner part, as shown above. Close up the canister.

8 Finish your front section by gluing **a** to the open side of the shutter mechanism you made on pages 22-23.

9 Glue the sides to the bottom and glue the frame to the top. The hole in the top is diagonally opposite the hole in the bottom.

10 Place your film in the middle section. Slot the frame in front of the film and stick the top to the sides with double-sided tape.

11 Stick the back, middle, and front sections together with electrical tape. Make a frame for your lens with small pieces of thin balsa wood.

12 Stick the lens to the front of your camera with double-sided tape. Tape over all joints and insert the winder in place.

Ready to go!
Glue the nut to the bottom or side of your camera so that you can put it on a tripod and tape over the hole at the bottom of your camera. You are now ready to take photos.

Between each shot, you will need to wind the key about one-and-a-half turns. When you have finished your film, take your camera into a dark room. In red light, take off the tape covering the bottom hole and use the key to wind the film back into the original canister. You will need to undo the tape to unload and reload your camera.

26 The Aperture

The aperture is the hole that the shutter uncovers when you take a picture. On many camera lenses, the size of the aperture is changed using a ring marked with numbers called f-stops. As the f-stop numbers get lower (from f 5.6 to f 4, for example), the aperture gets larger, letting more light into the camera.

MAKE it WORK!
The camera you made on pages 24-25 has an aperture that cannot change size. With a little extra work you can convert this camera so that it has an aperture with three different settings. You will need to remove the lens from your camera before you start.

You will need
thin brass sheet
a craft knife
stiff wire
scissors
a drill
glue

1 With scissors, cut three brass strips $\frac{1}{2}$" x 3". With an adult's help, make three holes in one of the pieces $\frac{1}{8}$", $\frac{1}{4}$", and $\frac{3}{8}$" wide.

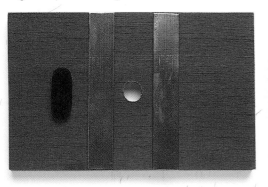

2 Glue the two blank strips of brass on either side of the hole, leaving enough space for the strip with holes.

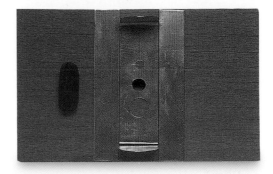

3 Position the center strip of brass as shown, so that it can slide up and down. Bend the ends of the brass strip away from the camera.

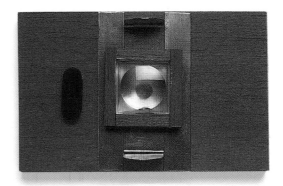

4 Fix the lens and frame back onto the camera, gluing the balsa wood to the two outer brass strips. The center strip should move freely. Bend the wire to form a viewfinder and attach this to the front of the camera with tape.

Varying your aperture

On page 23, we saw why you might want to let less light into the camera by using a quicker shutter speed. When would you want to let less light into the camera using the aperture? Using a standard 35-mm camera, you can see the effects of adjusting the aperture.

You will need

a camera with a variable aperture and shutter
colored cardboard numbers as below
six 2″ lengths of stiff wire   clay

1 Fix the numbers on wire and stick each one into clay. Position the numbers at different distances in front of your camera. Make sure all six numbers are in view.

2 Take photographs at different f-stops. You should focus on the nearest number each time. As you make the aperture smaller, you will need to use a slower shutter speed so that enough light enters the camera. If you are taking the pictures indoors, you may need to use a flash.

▶ With a large aperture, only the numbers nearest the camera are in focus. As the aperture gets smaller, more numbers appear in focus. With the smallest aperture, all the numbers are in focus. We can see that a small aperture gives a greater **depth of field**.

Using the aperture and shutter together

If you make the aperture bigger by one setting, the amount of light entering the camera doubles. If you make the shutter speed faster by one setting, the amount of light entering the camera halves. To photograph a moving scene without blurring your image, it is best to use a fast shutter speed and a large aperture. For a shot that needs a good depth of field, use a small aperture and a slower shutter speed.

The muscles in your eye work in a very similar way to the aperture in an automatic camera. Your pupil is a hole that lets light into your eye. When you walk into a dark room, the muscles in your eye make your pupil larger. This lets more light into your eye. When you look at a bright light, your pupil gets smaller.

▲ f 1.8

▲ f 2.8

▲ f 5.6

▲ f 22

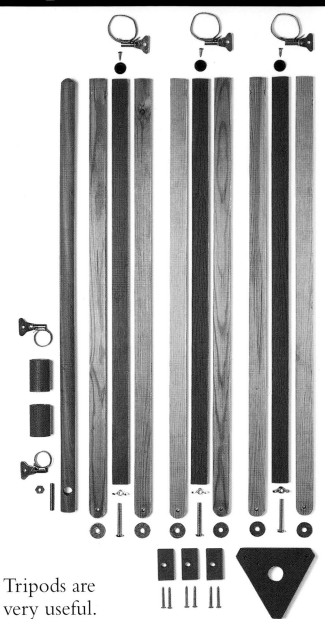

Tripods are very useful.

They hold cameras steady so that you can take photographs needing long exposures. At night, for example, you need to allow more time to let light into the camera. A tripod also supports your camera if you want to take a series of photographs from the same position.

MAKE it WORK!

Make a simple tripod for your pinhole camera or any camera that has a $1/4''$ threaded hole. Ask an adult to help you cut and drill the pieces.

You will need

$1^{1}/_{2}''$ dia. cardboard tube   three rubber washers
a wooden dowel $3/4'' \times 28''$ six metal washers
nine $1'' \times 3/8''$ wood strips: a hacksaw
   three $25^{1}/_{2}''$ long, six $27^{1}/_{2}''$ long   plywood
three $2''$ long bolts with wing nuts   screws
a $1^{1}/_{2}''$ long headless bolt and a $3/8''$ nut   a drill
two small hose clamps to fit around $3/4''$ dia.
three large hose clamps to fit around $1^{1}/_{4}''$ dia.

1 With a hacksaw, round off one end of the six $27^{1}/_{2}''$ strips. Drill a hole in each, $3/16''$ from the rounded end. Cut a plywood triangle with $4^{3}/_{4}''$ sides. Drill a $1''$ central hole and six smaller holes, as shown left.

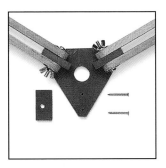 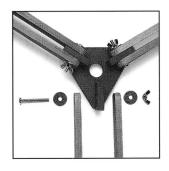

2 Cut three $3/4'' \times 1^{1}/_{2}''$ plywood rectangles, drilling a hole, off center, in each. Place a rectangle on its side so the hole is nearer to you than to the triangle. Screw the pieces together.

3 Sandwich the rectangle of wood between two of the round-ended strips and secure with a bolt, washers, and a wing nut.

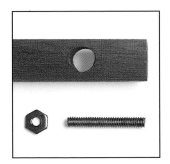 

4 Drill a $3/8''$ hole $3/4''$ from one end of the dowel. Drill a hole through the center of the dowel big enough for the bolt. Push the nut into the hole and screw in the bolt.

5 Push the dowel through the hole in the center of the triangle. Add two pieces of cardboard tube, 1$\frac{1}{2}$″ long, one on either side of the triangle. Move the dowel to the height that you want and fix it in place by tightening the two small hose clamps either side of the tubes.

6 Slot a 25$\frac{1}{2}$″ wooden strip in the middle of each tripod leg. Fix in place with a large hose clamp at the bottom. Now you can vary the height of the tripod by moving the center wood strips up or down and tightening the hose clamps.

7 Complete your tripod by screwing rubber washers to the bottom of each foot.

Using a tripod

Attach a camera to your tripod and try a simple **time-lapse photography** experiment. Ask a friend to blow up a balloon. Take a shot every couple of seconds to make a sequence as the balloon gets bigger. The tripod keeps your camera in position so that the photo frame does not change. You can make a zoetrope, as on pages 44-45, to **animate** the sequence.

By taking photographs of a plant at regular intervals during a day, botanists study how plants move and grow. They arrange these photographs in sequence and see how plants move to follow the sun.

When you are taking pictures outside, you can change the look of your photograph by standing with the sun behind you, in front of you, or to the side. You can light objects indoors in the same way to give different effects.

MAKE it WORK!

As you move a lamp around a collection of objects indoors, the changing shadows make the objects appear very different. Take photographs of your scenes using a tripod.

You will need

black and white cardboard
four medium binder clips
a desk lamp
clay
gels

1 Cut the cardboard to make the cone. Tape it together and fasten it to the lamp with clay. Ask an adult to check that your bulb is not too strong as this could cause the paper to get hot and even to burn.

2 Cardboard flaps give a wide band of light. To use them, take the cone off the lamp and attach two large squares of black cardboard to your lamp with the clips.

▲ back lighting: objects are lit from behind with the light pointing up from the floor

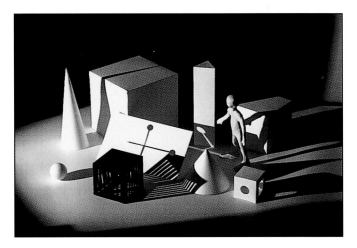

▲ side lighting: objects are lit from the left using the cardboard flaps

3 Make several boxes from the cardboard and model some shapes from clay as below.

Setting your scene

Place the objects on a table 3' from a wall. Light them using the cone to give a spotlight effect and the cardboard flaps to give a wide band of light. Change the appearance of the scene by lighting it from different angles.

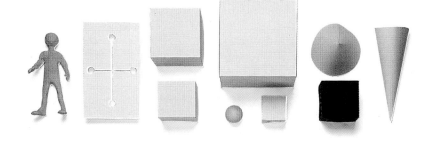

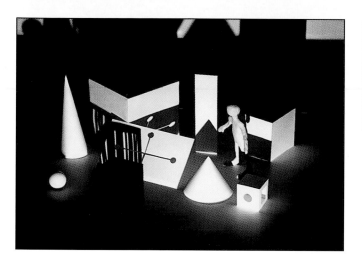

Looking at color
Investigate the effect of color by putting colored gels in between the objects and your light source. You can also use a projector to create an effect like the one shown at the bottom of this page.

▲ front lighting: objects are lit from the front using the cardboard flaps

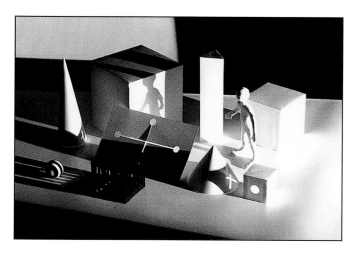

▲ side lighting: objects are lit from the right using the cardboard flaps

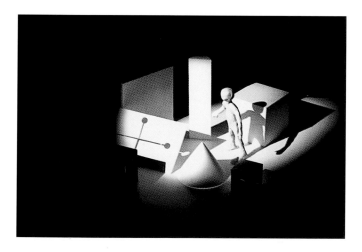

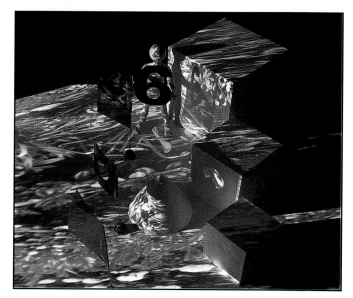

▲ spot lighting: objects are lit from the front using the cardboard cone

When film is exposed to light, chemical changes take place on the emulsion side. These changes form an imprint of the scene you have photographed. The image is invisible at this stage, so you need to process your film with chemicals in a light–proof tank in order to see the image.

Making your tank

1 Fold the rubber bands in half and loop them through the bulldog clips. Attach the rubber bands to the corks with the staples.

2 With an adult's help, drill a $^1/_2$″ hole near each end of the drainpipe.

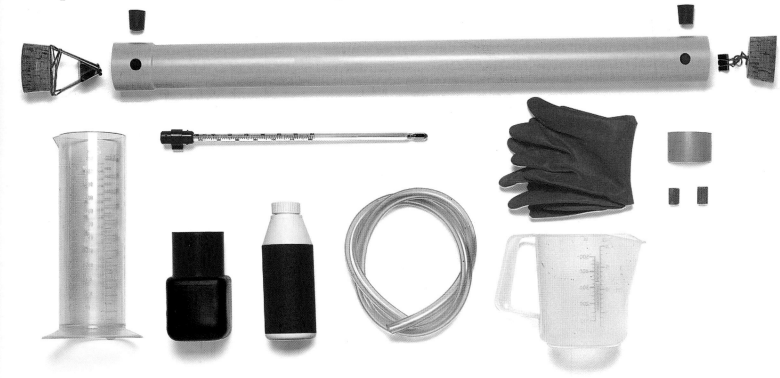

MAKE it WORK!

Make a processing tank to hold film and prepare your solutions: developer, fixer, and water, ready to process your own black and white film.

To prepare your tank and solutions you will need

two rubber bands	two bulldog clips 1″ wide
two fence staples	a thermometer
film processing solutions	rubber gloves
three measuring cylinders	a pitcher
two large corks to fit $2^1/_2$″ dia.	a saw
two balsa-wood strips $^1/_8$″ x 2″	a drill
30″ x $2^1/_2$″ dia. plastic drainpipe	glue
two rubber stoppers to fit $^1/_2$″ dia.	

3 To make a "light trap," ask an adult to help you saw a short piece of drainpipe in half lengthwise. Glue the balsa-wood strips inside one end of the tank on either side of the hole. Glue the underside of these strips. Slide in, and press on the piece of drainpipe.

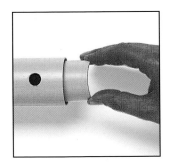 

Making up solutions

You need to dilute developer and fixer solutions before use. This means that you need to mix a small amount of each one with water. Ask an adult to help you prepare them. Always follow instructions for proper disposal of chemicals.

Be careful!

You can make up your solutions in the light in an ordinary room, but be careful not to splash them over you. Always wear rubber gloves and keep a window open nearby.

1 You will need to make about 16 fl. oz. of each solution. If, for example, the dilution is 1:7 for the developer, pour 2 fl. oz. of developer into the measuring cylinder.

2 Use a thermometer to check the temperature of the water. It should be a little warmer than recommended on the bottle so that when it is mixed with the cold developer, the solution will be the right temperature.

3 Add water to the developer. If the recommended dilution is 1:7, for example, add 14 fl. oz. to the 2 fl. oz. of developer. Now prepare your fixer solution to the recommended dilution. Then fill your third cylinder with water.

film reel

winder

tank

film canister

light-proof lids

Processing tanks

You can buy processing tanks that are more sophisticated than the one you have made. The tanks are light-proof and, once the film is inside and the top is in place, the chemicals can be poured into and out of the tank through the lid in normal room light.

MAKE it WORK!

Having made your tank and exposed a roll of film, you can now go into a darkroom and process your film. You can follow the steps shown below if you are using a commercial tank, too, but you will need to follow the manufacturer's instructions to load the film into the tank. Remember to take regular breaks outside the darkroom and to wear rubber gloves when you are pouring the solutions.

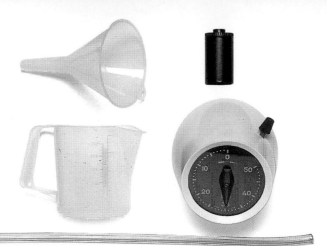

developer   water   fixer

You will need

your solutions: developer, fixer, and water

a funnel	a timer	scissors
a pitcher	a darkroom	a coin
plastic tubing	rubber gloves	
a hose clamp	an exposed film	
a sink or bucket	your processing tank	

What do the solutions do?

The developer changes the chemicals in the image area to produce an image you can see. After developing, you put the print in water to stop the image developing any more. The fixer makes the developed image permanent.

Processing a film

  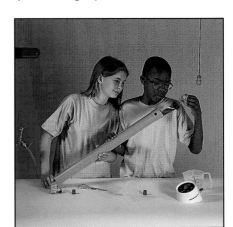

1 Arrange the equipment so that you can find the objects in the dark. It is a good idea to practice loading the tank in the light using an old piece of film.

2 Turn off the light and force open the top of your film roll using a coin. Cut off the narrow part off the film and attach the end to one of the bulldog clips.

3 Ease the film into the pipe. Push the cork into the end and let the film spool fall through to the other end of the pipe.

4 Cut the film at the other end of the pipe. Attach this end of the film to a bulldog clip in the same way as for the top. Push the cork into the end of the pipe.

5 Put a rubber stopper in the hole that does not have the light trap in place and turn on the safety light. Use a funnel to pour about 16 fl. oz. of developer into the other hole.

6 Put a stopper in this hole. Set the timer as recommended on your developer bottle. Gently rock the drainpipe to make sure that all parts of the film are covered by the solution.

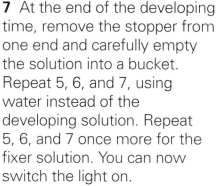

7 At the end of the developing time, remove the stopper from one end and carefully empty the solution into a bucket. Repeat 5, 6, and 7, using water instead of the developing solution. Repeat 5, 6, and 7 once more for the fixer solution. You can now switch the light on.

8 Attach the tubing to a cold tap with a hose clamp and pour water into the drainpipe to rinse the film. This takes about 10 minutes, so it's best to have your water emptying into a sink. If there is no sink nearby, empty the bucket as it fills up.

▶ To dry your film you can attach one end to a clothesline using a bulldog clip. Put another clip at the other end of the film so it doesn't curl up. When the film is dry, cut your negatives into strips and store them until you are ready to make prints.

The image on a piece of exposed photographic paper, such as the paper in a pinhole camera, is invisible. You need to develop the paper, as with film, in order to see the picture you have taken. A machine called an enlarger is used to shine light through negatives onto your paper to make prints.

MAKE it WORK!

In a darkroom, develop your own pinhole camera prints. Then use the negative prints to make positive images. You will need to use different solutions than those used to process a film.

You will need

a watch	a sink or bucket
rubber gloves	three plastic trays
a plastic funnel	a measuring cylinder
a thermometer	two pairs of plastic tongs
photographic solutions for developing prints	

Making up solutions

Ask an adult to help you dilute your solutions as on page 33. Fill your trays, $3/8''$ deep, with your solutions. Put developer in the first tray, water in the second, and fixer in the third. Before you start developing your print, read from the bottles how long you will need to leave the paper in each tray. Dispose of the used solutions properly.

Developing prints

1 Turn the safety light on. With gloves on, slide the paper into the developing tray for the recommended time.

2 Gently rock the tray so that the paper is covered evenly and the liquid is kept moving while developing.

3 When the time is up, remove the paper with tongs and drop it into the water for a few seconds. Gently rock as before.

 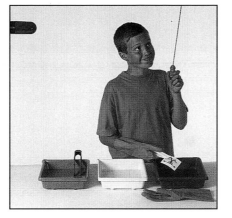 

4 Now slide the paper into the fixer tray for the recommended time and gently rock the tray.

5 Remove the print from the fixer and turn the room lights on.

6 Rinse the print in water in a sink or a bucket. Clip your print to a line and let it dry.

positive print

negative print

Making a positive print

1 With the safety light on, put the fresh photographic paper, emulsion (shiny) side up, on your surface.

2 Place the negative print, shiny side down, on top of the paper and cover with the glass to keep the sheets flat.

Your pinhole camera print

The developed print from your pinhole camera will be a negative image. You can use this negative to make a positive **contact print**. You will need some scissors, fresh photographic paper, photographic solutions, a flashlight, and a piece of glass with taped edges for safety. Again, you will need to do your work in a darkroom.

3 Shine a flashlight through the glass for five seconds. Develop the positive print in the same way as you developed the first print. If the image is not dark enough, try again with a longer exposure time.

38 Contact Sheets

Before taking the trouble to enlarge and print a negative you need to find the one that contains the best image. Contact sheets are positive prints made by placing negatives on photographic paper and shining light through them. From the contact sheet you can choose the best image and then go on to make an enlarged print.

MAKE it WORK!
You can take some shots of a clay figure, changing the settings of either the aperture or the shutter speed. Then you can make a contact sheet showing the same image at different light exposures.

You will need
photographic paper and a light-proof box
a camera with a variable aperture and
    shutter speed
black and white film for your camera
a piece of glass with taped edges
a darkroom
a tripod

1 First take a series of photographs of your object. Use a tripod to keep your camera steady. Keep either the shutter speed or aperture constant and take eight photographs, changing the other setting each time. Write down the settings as you go.

2 After processing, take your film into the darkroom. Turn the safety light on and place a sheet of photographic paper, shiny side up, on a clean surface.

3 Place the negatives, emulsion side down, onto the paper and cover with the sheet of glass.

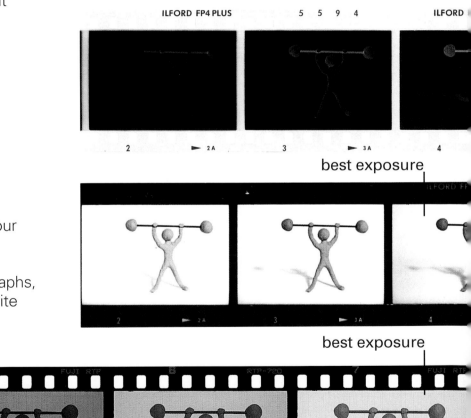

best exposure

best exposure

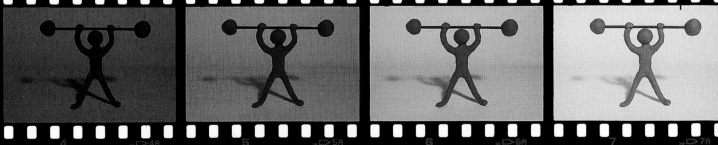

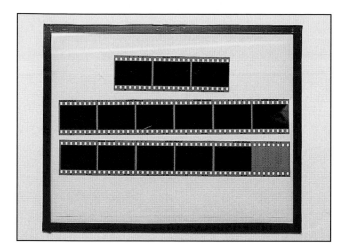

Many small cameras have been invented for use in surgery and espionage, but the smallest commercial camera is the round Japanese "Petal" camera. It has a diameter of $1^{1}/_{8}$" and a thickness of $^{5}/_{8}$". The largest and most expensive camera ever built is the $24^{1}/_{2}$ ton Rolls-Royce camera built in 1956. It is $8^{7}/_{8}$' wide and 46' long.

4 Turn the light on so that you expose the paper for a few seconds. Switch back to red light and put the paper into a light-proof box.

5 Develop your contact sheet using the technique used on pages 36-37.

Looking at your contact sheet

Choose the best image from the contact sheet and use the corresponding negative to make your print with an enlarger. Note the aperture and shutter settings used to produce the right exposure so you can use the setting next time.

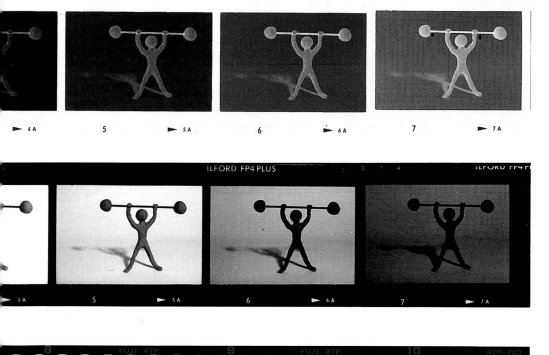

◀ On your negatives, the underexposed shots are quite light. The negatives are darker where the shots have been exposed to more light.

◀ You can see the same effect on the contact sheet, but, because these are positive images, the lights and darks are reversed.

◀ Transparency film gives a positive image. From a positive image you can identify the best exposure without making a contact sheet. To view a transparency, light is projected through it so that a large image is made on a screen.

The enlarger is a piece of equipment for making prints from film negatives. Light shines through the negative and projects a larger image onto a piece of photographic paper. With an enlarger you can make different-sized prints from the same negative. You can also improve your print by controlling the amount of light reaching some areas of the paper.

MAKE it WORK!

You can choose one of the negatives from which you made a contact sheet on pages 38-39 and enlarge it to make prints of different sizes. Enlargers are expensive machines, so you may need to join a photography club so you can use all the right equipment.

You will need

photographic paper and a light-proof box
scissors   a darkroom
negatives   a watch or timer
an enlarger   an adjustable easel

lamp

height adjuster

lens

negative holder

adjustable easel

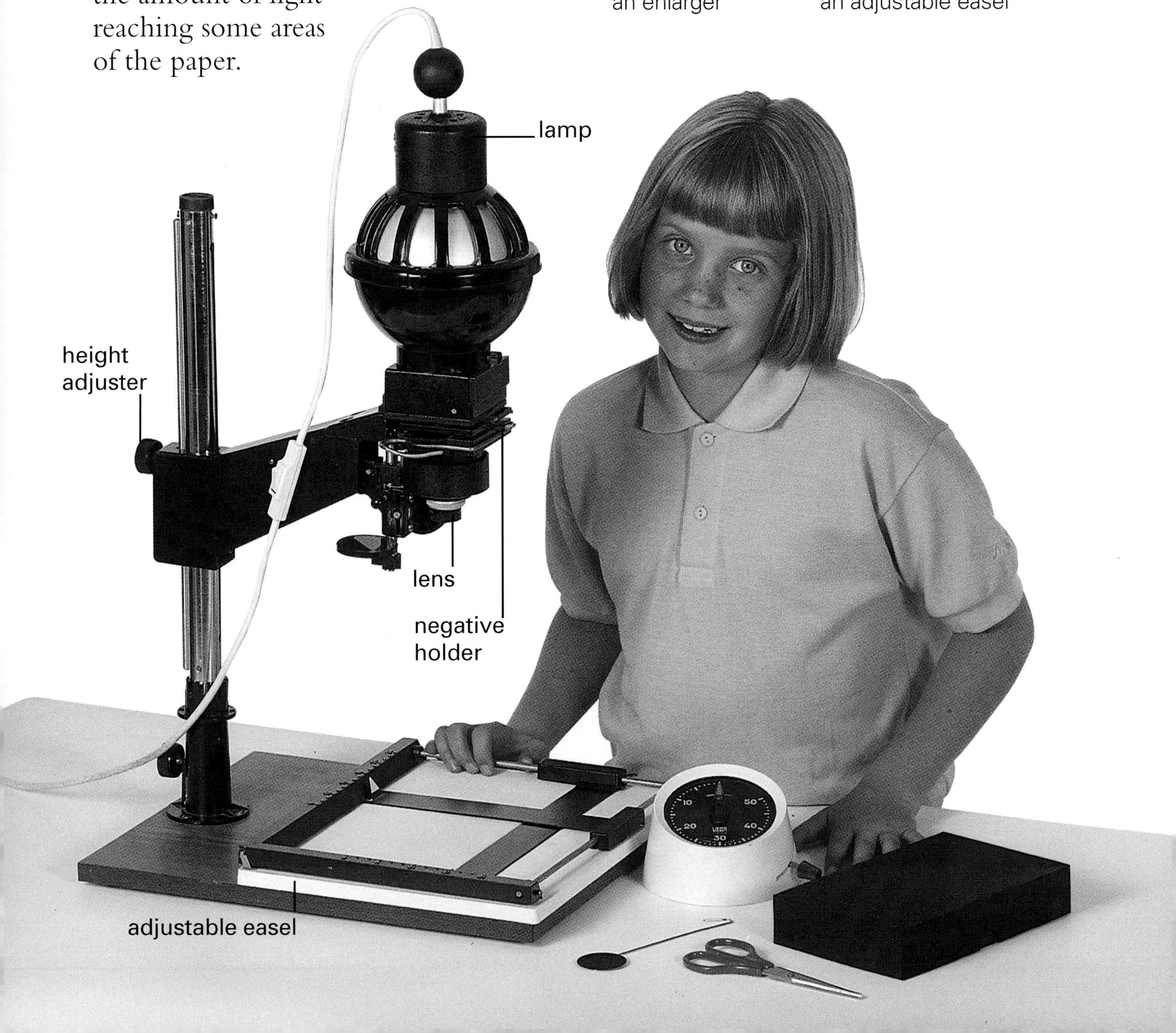

  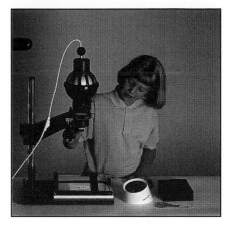

1 With the safety light on, put the negative strip in the holder so that the image you want to enlarge is centered in the frame.

2 Turn on the enlarger and adjust the height until the image on the easel is the size you want.

3 Now turn the focusing knob back and forth until the image on the easel is sharp. Now turn off the enlarger.

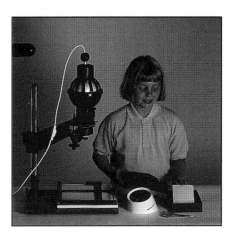 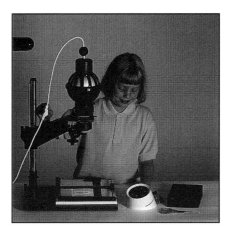

4 Take a sheet of photographic paper from its box. Position the paper on the easel so that the metal blades of the easel keep the paper in place.

5 Make a test strip, as below, to find the best exposure time. Turn the enlarger and timer on. When the time is up, put your paper in a box ready to develop.

Dodging and burning

You can lighten parts of a print by "dodging" over a dark area for some of the exposure time. Dodging stops light reaching this area. Make a dodging paddle by attaching a circle of black cardboard to stiff wire with tape. To darken areas, make a hole in a piece of black cardboard. After exposing the paper once, make a second exposure with the cardboard in place so that only the area needing extra light is exposed. This is known as "burning."

a dodging paddle

25 seconds   5 seconds

Making a test strip

You should make a test strip to find the ideal exposure time. To do this, use a piece of black cardboard to expose a narrow strip for five seconds. Move the cardboard back every five seconds to expose four or five further strips until all the paper is uncovered. When you develop the paper you will be able to see which exposure time gives the best print.

Photograms are pictures made without a camera. They are made when objects are placed on photographic paper that is then exposed to light. The objects stop light from reaching parts of the paper. So, when the paper is developed, an image of the objects is produced. You can use all sorts of everyday objects to create different effects.

MAKE it WORK!
Make photograms like the ones on these pages using photographic paper and some small objects.

You will need
photographic paper and a light-proof black box
small objects, e.g., clips, pins, pens, toys
a darkroom and safety light
a flashlight

1 Turn the safety light on and lay a piece of photographic paper shiny side up. Place your chosen objects on the paper and then shine the flashlight on the paper from above for about 10 seconds. If you are using flat objects you could make a test strip to find the ideal exposure time for your print, as shown on page 41. Be careful not to move the objects.

2 When you have finished exposing, put the paper in your black box until you are ready to develop your prints.

3 Follow the developing process described on pages 36-37.

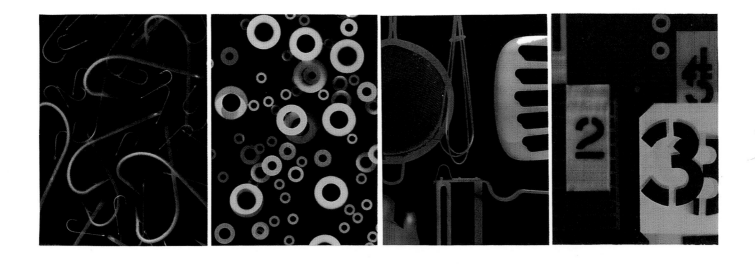

The first photograms were made in the middle of the 19th century. In Britain, Anna Atkins, thought to be the first woman photographer, made a beautiful handmade book of prints using this process. She used different types of seaweed to make blue negative prints, called cyanotypes.

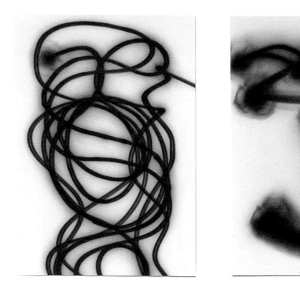

Experimenting with photograms

When you have made some photograms with opaque objects, try using objects that let some light through, such as pasta or flower petals, or transparent objects, such as a glass bowl or eyeglasses. Try shining the flashlight at an angle through a water glass. You can make double exposures by exposing the paper twice, using different objects each time.

Drawing with light

If you place a cone of cardboard over the end of the flashlight, you can use the beam of light that comes through as a "light pen." Draw several lines on different parts of the paper by turning the light off, moving it, and then turning it on again. The prints shown above have been made in this way.

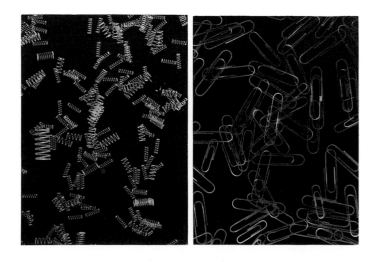

Using different grades of paper

Try making the same photogram on different grades of paper. The difference between paper grades lies in the number of shades of gray between white and black they can produce. A flat paper (grade 1) produces an image with lots of shades of gray. A high contrast (grade 5) gives the least number of tones and produces an image in black and white, with very few shades of gray.

Warning! Take care when handling sharp objects.

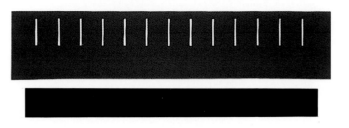

In the 19th century, before the invention of movies, people had toys called zoetropes. A zoetrope is a cylinder with slits that has pictures on the inside. When you spin the zoetrope around and look through the slits, it appears as if the pictures are moving.

MAKE it WORK!

You can make a zoetrope by making a cylinder and lining it with 13 contact prints that you have photographed and developed yourself.

You will need

black and yellow cardboard
a sequence of small prints
scissors and a craft knife
a plastic flowerpot
a pin

▲ Using wire and clay, you can make a figure to photograph.

1 Cut a strip of black cardboard the same length as your 13 prints placed next to each other. Cut another strip a little longer and twice as wide. Cut 13 slits equally spaced, as shown. The slits should be $3/16$" wide.

2 Glue the ends of the wide strip together to form a cylinder. You can put yellow cardboard over the bottom of the black cylinder to give it extra support. Cut a circular base the same size as the cylinder and tape it in place.

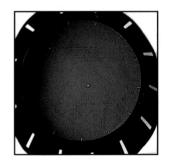

3 Push a pin through the center of the base and into the bottom of an upturned flowerpot.

4 Glue your series of prints along the narrow strip and glue this along the bottom edge of the inside of your cylinder.

Moving pictures

Sit on the floor and spin the cylinder. Look at the pictures through the slits. As the zoetrope moves around, the images should appear to move. You will need to experiment with the speed of your zoetrope to see what speed gives the best effect.

How do zoetropes work?

When you see a sequence of pictures at the rate of more than 13 frames per second, your brain puts the images together and you think you are seeing a moving scene. In movies and videos the images appear to move much more smoothly because 24 frames are shown every second.

The word "zoetrope" comes from the Greek meaning "wheel of life."

Animate To make separate pictures appear as if images are moving.

ASA ASA stands for the American Standards Association. It is a system of numbers used to describe the sensitivity of a film to light.

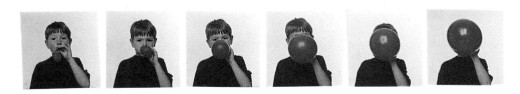

Concave lens A lens that bends light so that the beams of light travel away from each other.

Contact prints Prints made by shining light through a negative that is lying flat on a piece of photographic paper. A contact print is always the same size as its negative.

Contrast The difference between dark and light areas on prints and negatives, i.e., how many gray tones there are. A high contrast image has clear light and dark areas and few grays in between. A low contrast image has many gray tones and may seem "murky."

Convex lens A lens that bends light so that the beams of light meet at a point.

Crop To block out parts of an image that you don't want to print.

Depth of field In a photograph, the distance between the nearest point that is in focus and the farthest point that is also in focus is called the depth of field. If you take a photograph of two objects at different distances from you, both images are more likely to appear in focus if you use a small aperture.

Develop To use chemicals to see an image on photographic paper or film that has been exposed to light.

Dilute To make a liquid weaker by adding water to it.

Energy When something has energy it has the ability to make things move, change, or warm up. Flashlights and lamps change electricity into light energy, which can be detected by our eyes and photographic chemicals.

Expose To allow light to fall on photographic film or paper. In a camera an exposure is made when the shutter is open.

Field of view The field of view is how much you can see when you look through a camera. Different lenses, e.g., telephoto and wide angle, give you different fields of view.

Flash A device that produces a burst of light. It is used to make a dark scene brighter so that it can be recorded on film.

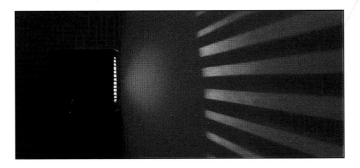

Focus To move a lens so that the image it produces is as clear and sharp as possible.

Gel A thin colored sheet of plastic that allows light of its own color to pass through, but that blocks out light of other colors.

Image A picture of something.

Inverted Turned upside down. An inverted image is one that appears upside down.

Lens A specially made piece of glass that can bend light.

Negative An image in which light and dark areas are reversed. The black areas appear white, and white areas appear black. A strip of developed negative film is called a "negative."

Opaque An object that is opaque does not allow light to pass through it. Metal, for example, is opaque.

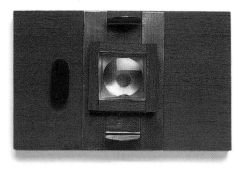

Overexposed Reached by too much light. An overexposed photograph is one taken with an exposure that lets too much light into the camera. Your printed positive image will be too light and some parts of the scene will be pure white.

Positive An image that has shades of black and white and color that are the same as that of the object.

Print An image that is recorded on photographic paper.

Reflect To bounce light back. We see objects because light beams reflect off them.

Refract To bend light. Some objects, such as lenses or jars of water, allow light to pass through them but cause the light to change direction.

Telephoto lens A lens that makes objects seem to be much nearer than they really are. It has a long focal length and a narrow field of view.

Time-lapse photography Photographs taken at different times and then put together to make a film. The effect is to show events that take place very slowly over hours or even days in just a few seconds.

Transparency film A type of film that gives a positive image. A slide is known as a transparency.

Transparent An object that is transparent allows light to pass through it.

Underexposed Not reached by enough light. An underexposed photograph is one taken with an exposure that doesn't allow enough light into the camera. Your printed positive image will be very dark.

Wide-angle lens A lens that has a wide field of view.